123726
5.1 B.L
.5 pts

EDGE BOOKS™

SPORTS RECORDS

THE GREATEST
FOOTBALL
RECORDS

BY TERRI DOUGHERTY

CONSULTANT:
Craig R. Coenen, PhD
Associate Professor of History
Mercer County Community College
West Windsor, New Jersey

Capstone
press®
Mankato, Minnesota

Edge Books are published by Capstone Press,
151 Good Counsel Drive, P.O. Box 669, Mankato, Minnesota 56002.
www.capstonepress.com

Library of Congress Cataloging-in-Publication Data
Dougherty, Terri.
    The greatest football records / by Terri Dougherty.
    p. cm. — (Edge books. Sports records)
    Summary: "Short stories and tables of statistics describe the history and greatest
records of the National Football League" — Provided by publisher.
    Includes bibliographical references and index.
    ISBN-13: 978-1-4296-2007-9 (hardcover)
    ISBN-10: 1-4296-2007-2 (hardcover)
    1. Football — United States — Miscellanea — Juvenile literature.
2. Football — Records — United States — Juvenile literature. 3. National
Football League. I. Title. II. Series.
GV950.7.D68 2009
796.332092 — dc22   2008002035

Editorial Credits
Aaron Sautter, editor; Bobbi J. Wyss, designer; Jo Miller, photo researcher

Photo Credits
AP Images/Morry Gash, cover (top left); Phil Sandlin, 10; Steve Hamm, 12;
    Tannen Maury, cover (bottom right)
Corbis/Bettman, 4, 14
Getty Images Inc./Al Bello, 28; Bruce Bennett Studios, 6; David Drapkin, 20;
    David Stluka, 8; Drew Hallowell, 22; NFL, 7, 18; NFL/James Flores, 16;
    Ron Hanna, 26; Vernon Biever, 24
Shutterstock/Gary Paul Lewis, cover (bottom left); Mark Cinotti, cover (top right);
    Supri Suharjoto, cover (middle right)

Records in this book are current through the 2007 season.

1 2 3 4 5 6 13 12 11 10 09 08

TABLE OF CONTENTS

CHAPTER 1

RECORD-SETTING
EXCITEMENT

4

Tom Dempsey wore a special shoe on his kicking foot.

LEARN ABOUT
- One Big Kick
- League Mergers
- The Super Bowl

Sometimes the most unlikely people achieve the greatest records. Tom Dempsey was born without a right hand and only half of a right foot. But he still made it to the National Football League (NFL) as a kicker.

On November 8, 1970, Dempsey kicked a record 63-yard field goal for the New Orleans Saints. Many people didn't think anyone could kick a field goal that far. But despite his disability, Dempsey booted the ball through the goalpost to make NFL history.

THE NFL KICKS OFF

NFL players have been setting records ever since the NFL kicked off in 1920. At first, the league was called the American Professional Football Association. It had just 14 teams. They had names like the Dayton Triangles and the Akron Pros. The Pros were the league's first undefeated team and won the first league championship. The league changed its name to the National Football League in 1922.

EDGE FACT

Dempsey's record field goal stood alone for 28 years. Denver's Jason Elam tied the record against Jacksonville on October 25, 1998.

Bronko Nagurski was a powerful running back who dominated opposing defenses.

Professional football grew popular over the next several decades. Fans cheered for their favorite teams and players. The Chicago Bears were one of the NFL's most successful teams during the 1930s and 1940s. Led by the legendary Bronko Nagurski, the Bears were called the "Monsters of the Midway."

In 1946, the All-America Football Conference (AAFC) was formed to rival the NFL. But the small league didn't last long. In 1950, a few of the AAFC teams joined the NFL. The NFL was then divided into two divisions called the American Conference and the National Conference.

TODAY'S NFL

In 1960, another new league challenged the NFL. It was called the American Football League (AFL). The first Super Bowl was held in 1967. The AFL and NFL champions played each other in the Super Bowl for the world championship title. In 1970, the AFL and NFL merged into one league to form the NFL as it is today.

Since the merger, many records have been set or broken. Millions of fans watch their favorite teams and players compete each week. Every game brings new excitement. Fans never know when a record might be broken to make NFL history.

Green Bay Packers receiver Max McGee scored the first touchdown in Super Bowl I.

CHAPTER 2

FOOTBALL'S
GREATEST PLAYERS

LEARN ABOUT

- Legendary Receivers
- Record Runners
- Terrific Tacklers

Brett Favre (#4) broke the passing touchdown record against the Minnesota Vikings in 2007.

8

GREEN BAY'S GUNSLINGER

Green Bay Packers quarterback Brett Favre is one of the NFL's all-time greats. On September 30, 2007, he fired a bullet pass to Greg Jennings for a 16-yard touchdown. It was the 421st touchdown pass of his career, setting a new NFL record.

MOST CAREER PASSING YARDS

61,655	Brett Favre	Atlanta, Green Bay
61,361	Dan Marino	Miami
51,475	John Elway	Denver
49,325	Warren Moon	Houston, Minnesota, Seattle, Kansas City
47,003	Fran Tarkenton	Minnesota, New York Giants

MOST PASSING YARDS IN A SEASON

5,084	Dan Marino	Miami, 1984
4,830	Kurt Warner	St. Louis, 2001
4,806	Tom Brady	New England, 2007
4,802	Dan Fouts	San Diego, 1981
4,746	Dan Marino	Miami, 1986
4,717	Daunte Culpepper	Minnesota, 2004

MOST CAREER TOUCHDOWN PASSES

442	Brett Favre	Atlanta, Green Bay
420	Dan Marino	Miami
342	Fran Tarkenton	Minnesota, New York Giants
306	Peyton Manning	Indianapolis
300	John Elway	Denver

MOST TOUCHDOWN PASSES IN A SEASON

50	Tom Brady	New England, 2007
49	Peyton Manning	Indianapolis, 2004
48	Dan Marino	Miami, 1984
44	Dan Marino	Miami, 1986
41	Kurt Warner	St. Louis, 1999

Few expected Favre to set NFL records. He played in only two games during his first season with the Atlanta Falcons. But things changed after being traded to the Packers in 1992. He led the team to a Super Bowl win in January 1997 and back to the Super Bowl again the next year. In 2007, Favre also set records for most career passing yards and most games won.

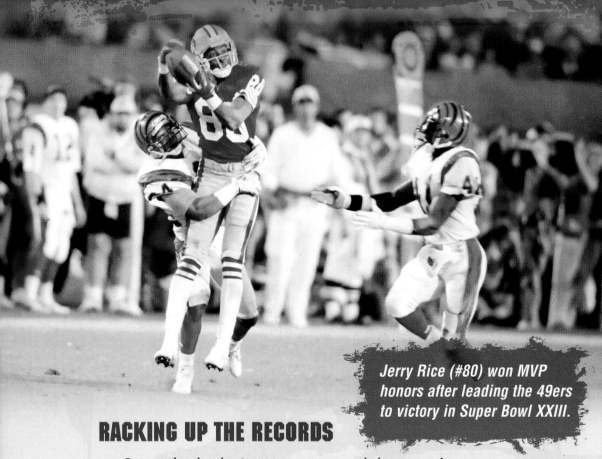

Jerry Rice (#80) won MVP honors after leading the 49ers to victory in Super Bowl XXIII.

RACKING UP THE RECORDS

Quarterbacks don't score many touchdowns without receivers to catch the ball. Jerry Rice is the greatest receiver in NFL history. In 1989, Rice pulled in pass after pass from San Francisco 49ers quarterback Joe Montana in Super Bowl XXIII. Rice set a Super Bowl record with 215 receiving yards. He was also the game's Most Valuable Player (MVP) as the 49ers beat the Cincinnati Bengals 20-16.

Rice played from 1985 to 2004. He caught 1,549 passes, more than any other receiver. He also shattered the record for the most receiving touchdowns, scoring 197. When he retired, he held 38 different NFL records.

MOST CAREER RECEIVING YARDS

22,895	Jerry Rice	San Francisco, Oakland, Seattle
14,934	Tim Brown	Los Angeles/Oakland Raiders, Tampa Bay
14,109	Isaac Bruce	Los Angeles/St. Louis Rams
14,004	James Lofton	Green Bay, L.A. Raiders, Buffalo, L.A. Rams, Philadelphia
13,944	Marvin Harrison	Indianapolis
13,899	Cris Carter	Philadelphia, Minnesota, Miami

MOST RECEIVING YARDS IN A SEASON

1,848	Jerry Rice	San Francisco. 1995
1,781	Isaac Bruce	St. Louis, 1995
1,746	Charley Hennigan	Houston, 1961
1,722	Marvin Harrison	Indianapolis, 2002
1,696	Torry Holt	St. Louis, 2003

MOST CAREER RECEIVING TOUCHDOWNS

197	Jerry Rice	San Francisco, Oakland, Seattle
130	Cris Carter	Philadelphia, Minnesota, Miami
129	Terrell Owens	San Francisco, Philadelphia, Dallas
124	Randy Moss	Minnesota, Oakland, New England
123	Marvin Harrison	Indianapolis

MOST RECEIVING TOUCHDOWNS IN A SEASON

23	Randy Moss	New England, 2007
22	Jerry Rice	San Francisco, 1987
18	Mark Clayton	Miami, 1984
18	Sterling Sharpe	Green Bay, 1994

MOST CAREER RECEPTIONS

1,549	Jerry Rice	San Francisco, Oakland, Seattle
1,101	Cris Carter	Philadelphia, Minnesota, Miami
1,094	Tim Brown	Los Angeles/Oakland Raiders, Tampa Bay
1,042	Marvin Harrison	Indianapolis

MOST RECEPTIONS IN A SEASON

143	Marvin Harrison	Indianapolis, 2002
123	Herman Moore	Detroit, 1995
122	Cris Carter	Minnesota, 1994
122	Cris Carter	Minnesota, 1995
122	Jerry Rice	San Francisco, 1995

RUSHING INTO HISTORY

Great running backs are the backbone of many strong offenses. On October 27, 2002, Emmitt Smith grabbed the football and burst through the Dallas Cowboys' offensive line. He ran for 11 yards and into NFL history. With that simple play, he became the NFL's all-time leading rusher.

Smith's great running helped the Cowboys win three Super Bowls in four years during the 1990s. He retired in 2004 with 18,355 total rushing yards, more than any other running back. He also holds an amazing record of 164 rushing touchdowns.

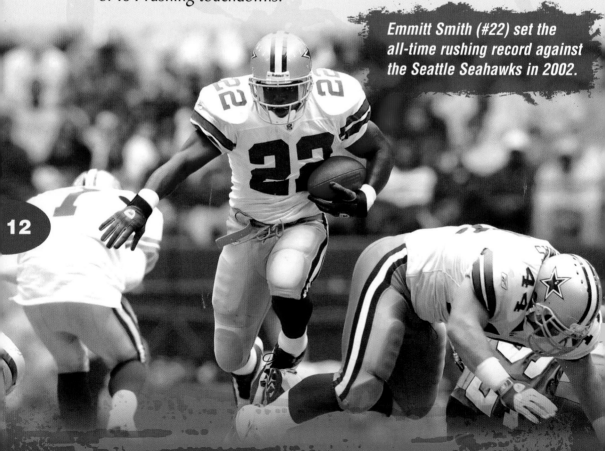

Emmitt Smith (#22) set the all-time rushing record against the Seattle Seahawks in 2002.

MOST CAREER RUSHING YARDS

18,355	Emmitt Smith	Dallas, Arizona
16,726	Walter Payton	Chicago
15,269	Barry Sanders	Detroit
14,101	Curtis Martin	New England, New York Jets
13,662	Jerome Bettis	Los Angeles/St. Louis Rams, Pittsburgh

MOST RUSHING YARDS IN A SEASON

2,105	Eric Dickerson	Los Angeles Rams, 1984
2,066	Jamal Lewis	Baltimore, 2003
2,053	Barry Sanders	Detroit, 1997
2,008	Terrell Davis	Denver, 1998
2,003	O. J. Simpson	Buffalo, 1973

MOST CAREER RUSHING TOUCHDOWNS

164	Emmitt Smith	Dallas, Arizona
123	Marcus Allen	Los Angeles Raiders, Kansas City
115	LaDainian Tomlinson	San Diego
110	Walter Payton	Chicago
106	Jim Brown	Cleveland

MOST RUSHING TOUCHDOWNS IN A SEASON

28	LaDainian Tomlinson	San Diego, 2006
27	Priest Holmes	Kansas City, 2003
27	Shaun Alexander	Seattle, 2005
25	Emmitt Smith	Dallas, 1995
24	John Riggins	Washington, 1983

EDGE FACT

On November 4, 2007, Minnesota Vikings running back Adrian Peterson set a record that will be hard to beat. In his first NFL season, Peterson set the single-game rushing record of 296 yards against the San Diego Chargers.

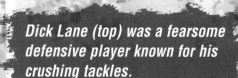

Dick Lane (top) was a fearsome defensive player known for his crushing tackles.

"NIGHT TRAIN" STEAMS AHEAD

Teams don't win games with offense alone. They also need a strong defense. Dick "Night Train" Lane was one of the best defensive players of all time.

During his **rookie** season in 1952, Lane caught a record 14 **interceptions**. Lane was a fast player who often beat receivers to the ball. He was also a star tackler. Lane played for the Los Angeles Rams, Chicago Cardinals, and Detroit Lions. He retired in 1965 after 14 NFL seasons. Lane's interception record still stands as the most in a single season.

rookie — a first-year player
interception — a pass caught by a defensive player

MOST INTERCEPTIONS IN A SEASON

14	Dick Lane	Los Angeles, 1952
13	Dan Sandifer	Washington, 1948
13	Orban Sanders	New York Yanks, 1950
13	Lester Hayes	Oakland, 1980

MOST CAREER INTERCEPTIONS

81	Paul Krause	Washington, Minnesota
79	Emlen Tunnell	New York Giants, Green Bay
71	Rod Woodson	Pittsburgh, San Francisco, Baltimore, Oakland

MOST INTERCEPTIONS BY A ROOKIE IN A SEASON

14	Dick Lane	Los Angeles, 1952
13	Dan Sandifer	Washington, 1948
12	Woodley Lewis	Los Angeles, 1950
12	Paul Krause	Washington, 1964

MOST CAREER SACKS

200.0	Bruce Smith	Buffalo, Washinton
198.0	Reggie White	Philadelphia, Green Bay, Carolina
160.0	Kevin Green	Los Angeles Rams, Pittsburgh, Carolina, San Francisco

MOST SACKS IN A SEASON

22.5	Michael Strahan	New York Giants, 2001
22.0	Mark Gastineau	New York Jets, 1984
21.0	Reggie White	Philadelphia, 1987
21.0	Chris Doleman	Minnesota, 1989

EDGE FACT

In 2001, Michael Strahan's record of 22.5 sacks caused a stir. When Strahan sacked quarterback Brett Favre, he broke Mark Gastineau's old record of 22. But some people believe Favre let himself be sacked so his friend Strahan could get the record.

CHAPTER 3

FOOTBALL'S
GREATEST TEAMS

LEARN ABOUT

- Super Teams
- A Huge Comeback
- Big-Time Scoring

Bart Starr (#15) led the Green Bay Packers to five NFL championships in the 1960s.

GREEN BAY'S GLORY DAYS

16

During the 1960s, the Green Bay Packers were one of the greatest teams to play the game. In 1960, the Packers came within 8 yards of winning the NFL championship game. But they came up short in a 17-13 loss to the Philadelphia Eagles. It was the only postseason game Vince Lombardi lost as the Packers head coach.

MOST LEAGUE CHAMPIONSHIPS

12	Green Bay Packers	1929–1931, 1936, 1939, 1944, 1961–62, 1965–67, 1996
9	Chicago Bears	1921, 1932–33, 1940–41, 1943, 1946, 1963, 1985
7	New York Giants	1927, 1934, 1938, 1956, 1986, 1990, 2007

MOST SUPER BOWL VICTORIES

5	Dallas Cowboys	1971, 1977, 1992, 1993, 1995
5	Pittsburgh Steelers	1974, 1975, 1978, 1979, 2005
5	San Francisco 49ers	1981, 1984, 1988, 1989, 1994

The next year, quarterback Bart Starr led the Packers to win the 1961 championship game. The team went on to win championships in 1962, 1965, 1966, and 1967.

To reach the 1968 Super Bowl, the Packers first faced the Dallas Cowboys in the 1967 NFL championship game. Due to the bone-chilling temperatures in Green Bay, the game is famously called "The Ice Bowl." At game time, it was minus 13 degrees Fahrenheit (minus 25 degrees Celsius). In the exciting finish, Starr sneaked into the end zone behind Jerry Kramer's block. The score gave the Packers a 21-17 win over Dallas and their second straight trip to the Super Bowl. Starr's famous play was the highlight of a record five championships in seven years.

EDGE FACT

The Buffalo Bills are the only team to reach the Super Bowl four years in a row. However, they lost every time. They were beaten by the New York Giants, Washington Redskins, and twice by the Dallas Cowboys.

MIAMI REACHES PERFECTION

No team has ever had a season like the 1972 Miami Dolphins. During the regular season, the Dolphins rolled to a 14-0 record. The pressure was on as the playoffs began. Nobody was sure if the team could remain unbeaten and make it to Super Bowl VII. But after two come-from-behind victories against Cleveland and Pittsburgh, the Dolphins made it to the championship game.

Running back Larry Csonka (#39) helped carry the 1972 Dolphins to a perfect record.

SINGLE-SEASON RECORDS, INCLUDING PLAYOFFS

17-0	Miami Dolphins	1972
18-1	New England Patriots	2007
18-1	Chicago Bears	1985
18-1	San Francisco 49ers	1984

MOST CONSECUTIVE WINS, REGULAR SEASON

19	New England Patriots	2006–2007
18	New England Patriots	2003–2004
17	Chicago Bears	1933–1934
16	Chicago Bears	1941–1942
16	Miami Dolphins	1971–1973
16	Miami Dolphins	1983–1984
16	Pittsburgh Steelers	2004–2005

Miami coach Don Shula had already lost two Super Bowls. He badly wanted to win Super Bowl VII. At first it seemed Miami would have no problem against the Washington Redskins. The Dolphins were ahead 14-0 late in the fourth quarter when the Redskins scored a touchdown on a blocked field goal. It looked like Washington could have a huge comeback win. But Miami hung on to win 14-7. The Dolphins became the first team in NFL history to finish unbeaten and untied.

EDGE FACT

The 2007 New England Patriots came close to matching the Dolphins' achievement. They won every game that season, but lost in the Super Bowl to the New York Giants.

Quarterback Frank Reich (#14) and kicker Steve Christie (#2) led the Bills to the NFL's biggest comeback win in 1993.

THE GREATEST RALLY

Sometimes teams have to fight hard to get a win. During a 1993 playoff game, the Houston Oilers were leading the Buffalo Bills 35-3. It looked like they were sure to win. But a game isn't over until the clock runs out. Buffalo chipped away at Houston's lead. In the second half, the Bills **rallied** to score 35 points and take a 38-35 lead.

rally — to come from behind to tie or take the lead

BIGGEST REGULAR SEASON COMEBACK WINS

28 POINTS BEHIND	San Francisco 38, New Orleans 35
	December 7, 1980, at San Francisco
26 POINTS BEHIND	Buffalo 37, Indianapolis 35
	September 21, 1991, at Buffalo
25 POINTS BEHIND	St. Louis 31, Tampa Bay 28
	November 8, 1987, at St. Louis

GREATEST POSTSEASON COMEBACKS

32 POINTS BEHIND	Buffalo 41, Houston 38
	January 3, 1993, at Buffalo
24 POINTS BEHIND	San Francisco 39, New York Giants 38
	January 5, 2003, at San Francisco
20 POINTS BEHIND	Detroit 31, San Francisco 27
	December 22, 1957, at San Francisco

The Oilers managed to kick a field goal to tie the game. But the Bills kicked their own field goal to win in overtime. Their 41-38 victory was the greatest comeback win in NFL history. The Bills went on to play in their third straight Super Bowl.

EDGE FACT

Tennessee Titans kicker Rob Bironas kicked a record eight field goals against the Houston Texans on October 21, 2007. He made the game-winner as time ran out to give the Titans a 38-36 victory.

SCORING MACHINES

Putting lots of points on the scoreboard is usually a sure way to win. The 1998 Minnesota Vikings had this mastered. Receivers Randy Moss and Cris Carter hauled in passes from quarterback Randall Cunningham all season. The team was almost unstoppable. Minnesota set an NFL record with 556 points on the way to a 15-1 record.

Randy Moss led both the 1998 Vikings and the 2007 Patriots to record scoring seasons.

MOST POINTS, REGULAR SEASON

589	New England	2007
556	Minnesota	1998
541	Washington	1983
540	St. Louis	2000

MOST TOTAL POINTS IN A GAME

113	Washington (72) vs. New York Giants (41)	November 27, 1966
106	Cincinnati (58) vs. Cleveland (48)	November 28, 2004
101	Oakland (52) vs. Houston (49)	December 22, 1963
96	Cleveland (51) vs. Cincinnati (45)	September 16, 2007

MOST YARDS GAINED, SEASON

7,075	St. Louis	2000
6,936	Miami	1984
6,800	San Francisco	1998
6,580	New England	2007

FEWEST POINTS ALLOWED, 16-GAME SEASON

165	Baltimore Ravens	2000
187	Chicago Bears	1986
191	Tennessee Titans	2000

In 2007, the New England Patriots broke the Vikings' record for the most points in a season. They scored 589 points that year. Randy Moss was a member of both record-setting teams.

EDGE FACT

The Chicago Bears crushed the Washington Redskins 73-0 in the 1940 NFL championship game. It was the most points ever scored by one team in an NFL game.

CHAPTER 4

FOOTBALL'S
WILDEST RECORDS

LEARN ABOUT
- A Big Mistake
- One Long Game
- A Historic Night

Jim Marshall (#70) was a big part of the Vikings' "Purple People Eaters" defense in the 1970s.

"WRONG WAY" AND "IRON MAN"

Even great NFL players sometimes make mistakes. On October 25, 1964, Jim Marshall picked up a fumble and ran into the end zone. He thought he had scored a touchdown for the Minnesota Vikings. Instead, he scored a **safety** for the other team. He ran the wrong way!

safety — a two-point score made by keeping a team from moving the ball out of its own end zone

24

CONSECUTIVE GAMES PLAYED, NON-SPECIAL TEAMS

282	Jim Marshall	Cleveland, Minnesota
253	Brett Favre	Green Bay
240	Mick Tingelhoff	Minnesota
229	Bruce Matthews	Houston/Tennessee
210	Jim Otto	Oakland

MOST SEASONS PLAYED

26	George Blanda	1949–58, 1960–75
25	Morten Andersen	1982–04, 2006–07
23	Gary Anderson	1982–2004

MOST SEASONS PLAYED WITH ONE TEAM

20	Jackie Slater	Los Angeles/St. Louis Rams 1976–1995
20	Darrell Green	Washington Redskins 1983–2002
19	Jim Marshall	Minnesota Vikings 1961–1979
19	Bruce Matthews	Houston Oilers/Tennessee Titans 1983–2001
18	Jim Hart	St. Louis Cardinals 1966–1983
18	Jeff Van Note	Atlanta Falcons 1969–1986
18	Pat Leahy	New York Jets 1974–1991

Marshall earned the nickname "Wrong Way" for his wrong-way run. But he holds an impressive record as well. From 1960 to 1979, he played in 282 consecutive games. He played 20 straight years for the Vikings without missing a single game. Marshall was truly the "Iron Man" of the NFL.

EDGE FACT

In 2000, the Baltimore Ravens' defense had a record-breaking year. They set a record for fewest points allowed in a 16-game season with just 165. The Ravens' dominant defense carried the team into the playoffs and victory in Super Bowl XXXV.

Chiefs kicker Jan Stenerud (#3) missed a possible game-winning field goal against the Dolphins in 1971.

THE LONGEST GAME

If an NFL game ends in a tie, the game goes into overtime. The first team to score wins the game. But what happens if the game is still tied at the end of overtime? During the regular season, the game is recorded as a tie. But in the playoffs, teams keep playing until there is a winner. That's what happened in the 1971 playoff game between the Kansas City Chiefs and the Miami Dolphins.

LONGEST OVERTIMES IN NFL HISTORY

22:40	Miami Dolphins 27, Kansas City Chiefs 24	December 25, 1971
17:54	Dallas Texans 20, Houston Oilers 17	December 23, 1962
17:02	Cleveland Browns 23, New York Jets 20	January 3, 1987
15:43	Oakland Raiders 37, Baltimore Colts 31	December 24, 1977
15:10	Carolina Panthers 29, St. Louis Rams 23	January 10, 2004

MOST TIE GAMES IN A SEASON

6	Chicago Bears	1932
5	Frankford Yellow Jackets	1929
4	Chicago Bears	1924
4	Orange Tornadoes	1929
4	Portsmouth Spartans	1932

The teams traded the lead throughout the game on December 25. With 35 seconds left in the game, the Chiefs' Jan Stenerud tried to win it with a field goal. He missed, and the score was tied 24-24.

Neither team could score in overtime. The game had to go into double overtime. Finally, halfway through the sixth quarter, Garo Yepremian kicked a 37-yard field goal. Miami won 27-24. At 82 minutes and 40 seconds, it was the longest professional football game ever played.

EDGE FACT

No one scored when the Detroit Lions played the New York Giants on November 7, 1943. No NFL game has ended in a 0-0 tie since.

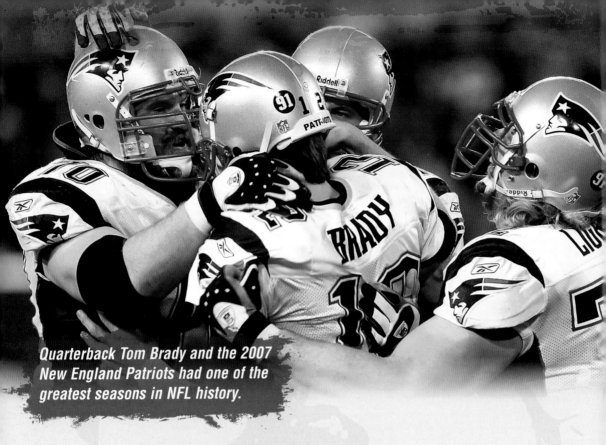

Quarterback Tom Brady and the 2007 New England Patriots had one of the greatest seasons in NFL history.

ONE FOR THE HISTORY BOOKS

December 29, 2007, was one of the most incredible nights in the history of the NFL. The New England Patriots were going for an undefeated season. But the New York Giants weren't making it easy. In the fourth quarter, the Patriots were behind and needed to score. Quarterback Tom Brady knew who would be open. Running down the sideline was receiver Randy Moss. He had his defender beat. Brady heaved the ball to Moss, who caught it in stride and ran 65 yards for a touchdown. The Patriots won the game 38-35.

LONGEST RUN FROM SCRIMMAGE

99 YARDS	Tony Dorsett	Dallas vs. Minnnesota, January 2, 1983
98 YARDS	Ahman Green	Green Bay vs. Denver, December 28, 2003
97 YARDS	Andy Uram	Green Bay vs. Chicago Cardinals, October 8, 1939
97 YARDS	Bob Gage	Pittsburgh vs. Chicago Bears, December 4, 1949

LONGEST INTERCEPTION RETURN

106 YARDS	Ed Reed	Baltimore vs. Cleveland, November 7, 2004
103 YARDS	Vencie Glenn	San Diego vs. Denver, November 29, 1987
103 YARDS	Louis Oliver	Miami vs. Buffalo, October 4, 1992

LONGEST RETURN OF MISSED FIELD GOAL

109 YARDS	Antonio Cromartie	San Diego vs. Minnesota, November 4, 2007
108 YARDS	Devin Hester	Chicago vs. New York Giants, November 12, 2006
108 YARDS	Nathan Vasher	Chicago vs. San Francisco, November 13, 2005
107 YARDS	Chris McAlister	Baltimore vs. Denver, September 30, 2002
104 YARDS	Aaron Glenn	New York Jets vs. Indianapolis, November 15, 1998

That one toss broke two NFL records. Brady set the record for the most touchdown passes in a season, with 50. Moss set a new record for the most touchdown catches in a season, with 23.

The Patriots broke more records that night too. They scored the most points by any team in a single season. And they were the first team to go 16-0 in the regular season. Amazingly, the Patriots lost the Super Bowl that season against the same Giants team they had just beaten. But the 2007 Patriots will still be remembered as one of the greatest NFL teams of all time.

GLOSSARY

field goal (FEELD GOHL) — a three-point score made by kicking the ball through the goalposts

fumble (FUHM-buhl) — to drop the football while running with it

interception (in-tur-SEP-shun) — a pass caught by a defensive player

overtime (OH-vur-time) — an extra period played if the score is tied at the end of four quarters

rally (RAL-ee) — to come from behind to tie or take the lead

rookie (RUK-ee) — a first-year player

sack (SAK) — when a defensive player tackles the opposing quarterback behind the line of scrimmage

safety (SAYF-tee) — a two-point score made by keeping a team from moving the ball out of its own end zone

touchdown (TUHCH-down) — a six-point score made by moving the ball over an opposing team's goal line

READ MORE

Giglio, Joe. *Great Teams in Pro Football History.* Great Teams. Chicago: Raintree, 2006.

Madden, John. *John Madden's Heroes of Football: The Story of America's Game.* New York: Dutton Children's Books, 2006.

Pellowski, Michael J. *The Little Giant Book of Football Facts.* New York: Sterling, 2005.

INTERNET SITES

FactHound offers a safe, fun way to find Internet sites related to this book. All of the sites on FactHound have been researched by our staff.

Here's how:
1. Visit *www.facthound.com*
2. Choose your grade level.
3. Type in this book ID **1429620072** for age-appropriate sites. You may also browse subjects by clicking on letters, or by clicking on pictures and words.
4. Click on the **Fetch It** button.

FactHound will fetch the best sites for you!

INDEX